Where Can We Go From Here?

written by Nancy Louise Spinelle
illustrated by K.J. Torda

We can go up the hill,

over the bridge,

then down the road.
Where can we go from here?

We can go under the fence,

through the field,

and across the ditch.
Where can we go from here?

We can go around the pond,

between the bushes,

past the shed,

and into the hole.

Home!